ARRIVAL

Arrival

Poems

Cynthia Anderson

Sheila-Na-Gig Editions

ISBN: 979-8-9873058-1-2
Library of Congress Control Number: 2022952401

Published by Sheila-Na-Gig Editions
Russell, KY
Hayley Mitchell Haugen, Editor
www.sheilanagigblog.com

ACKNOWLEDGMENTS

Many thanks to the journals where these poems first appeared, some in earlier versions.

Birds, Beasts and Trees: "The Linton Yew"
Cholla Needles: "Alcyone Retold," "Angry Stone," "Companion," "Encounter," "Gideon's Bluff," "Neolithic Girl," "Never Again," "Ode to a Pear," "The Last of Their Kind," "The Thing with Feathers," "Winter Solstice"
Crab Creek Review: "Golden Torch"
Dark Matter Women Witnessing: "Invoking the Salamander"
Failed Haiku: "Cosmic Soup," "Temps Perdu"
January Review: "A Long Goodbye"
Kosmos Quarterly: "Becoming Sequoia"
Lothlorien Poetry Journal: "For Helena," "Grandmother Returns to Sedona Through My Eyes," "River Daisies, River Geese"
MacQueen's Quinterly: "Doctor, My Eyes," "Trail Chains"
Mojave River Review: "Muir in the Woods"
Natural Inspirations: "Saltwater Woman"
Postcard Poetry and Prose: "The Shallows"
River Poets Journal: "Walking"
Santa Barbara Independent: "Sea Turtle"
Sheila-Na-Gig online: "Arrival," "Spring Equinox," "The Interior," "This Morning in the Foothills"
Silver Birch Press: "Overnight at White Pocket," "This Changes Everything"
Total Eclipse: "Blue Beetles"
Verse-Virtual: "Mourning the Doves," "Needed Elsewhere," "The Sanctity of Reading," "The Spinner"
Wend Poetry: "The Outer World"
Whale Road: "Seal Man"

As always, for Bill

CONTENTS

1: The Face of the World

II: Mapless

III: Mercy Seat

I.

The Face of the World

Walking

The sea air shines with moisture
as the sun warms a breeze off the water,
and I'm walking, the firm sand yielding
ever so slightly to my feet.

When I don't know what to do
I set off over beaches or trails
or streets. A procession of routes
winds down the years,
like favorite books in their places,
long unopened.

My mother believed in walking.
After my first steps,
she would take me to the post office,
a half block from home—
no stroller, no matter how long it took.

Maybe that's why I put
my faith in my feet—
and why I always understood
something about a wanderer
with a bundle.

I let my body move
when my mind couldn't.
Sooner or later,
I trusted my mind to follow...

> *Tree spirit*
> *Sea grass dweller*
> *Snake sliding into water*
> *Hawk wheeling away*

What I love more than anything
is the face of the world
turning toward me.

Spring Equinox

Last week yellow tape
cordoned a pile of rubble
on the beach, the remains
of a freshly fallen cliff.
But today, the equinox
upholds all desires, the way
fog and sun share the air
and rose petals scatter
on the littoral—the aftermath
of a wedding, followed
by another, and another
up and down the sand.
My friend says on this day
an egg will balance upright
on the ground—*Try it,* she says,
I have four in my yard.
But the cusp already
has everything I need—
love, chance meetings,
and memory threading
towards a magnetic pole.

Golden Torch

The sun is stingy
on the coast in June,
but finally, through the fog,
enough warmth seeps through,
and the golden torch bursts
into bloom.

From an old clay pot,
the spiny columns curve
gracefully upward, a sight
more at home in the desert
than here. Nearly every year
brings a bloom or two—
this year, three.

Each day we check the progress.
Dark furry nubs swell
to thick stems, then bud
into flowers big as plates—
tender petals shimmering
between the cream of camellia
and crystalline snow.

Inside, hundreds of tendrils
tipped with pale yellow
recede to the core, a deepening
lime green whorl, the end
of the known universe.

Slender stamens claim
the last triumph, rising
up and out to the sky,
calling the sun god
to make good on his promises.

And he answers.
A black bee, delirious,
enters the temple, sinks
on the soft gold carpet,
then staggers away with
his hoard of happiness.

The Spinner

Tentacles of silken thread
stretch from pot to pot
on the patio, and up
the stairs to succulents
on the sunlit ledges.
There, swaying in space,
sit the spiraled center and
its architect, an orange
clump big as a cat's eye,
legs drawn in, waiting,
as I bat the web apart.
The moorings stick
to my hands, and the more
I pull, the more the spider
reels out, until I finally see this,
and stop, and laugh—
for a moment letting go
of my fight with a foe's
deliberate designs
on my universe.

Saltwater Woman

she's at the littoral
where churning tides
wear away stone
making space
out of none

vibrant green
her long, fine hair
swirls everywhere
as waves rush
into her womb

all around her
starfish arms
anemone mouths
spiny urchins
drenched with spume

avatar of foam
she travels
the old way
star seed
of ancient days

she waits
until you're
mesmerized
enters your blood
and never leaves

Angry Stone

I walked in the mist
at Moonstone Beach
collecting pebbles
for potted cactuses
a treasure trove
of rainbow colors
shining as I filled
a bag or two

one red stone
stood out from the rest
as I held it
the thought arrived
to put it back
a thought that clung
until I knew
the stone had spoken

for a moment
I considered
taking it anyway
indulging
the human penchant
for power
that in the end
backfires

I carried the stone
a short way
then dropped it
because
it was angry
too angry
to ignore

The Outer World

Minerals give themselves
to weather, and skin
to whatever comes next.

My skeleton has
its own intelligence—
sometimes slow to move.

When I bend,
my skull, with its permanent
smile, pauses—

As do my spine,
my extravagant femurs,
my precious ulnas.

Flesh covers this frame
like lichen with only
rock to live on—

tenacious
in the fleeting light
of the outer world.

This Morning in the Foothills

A young deer leapt into the road
so unexpected it seemed he flew there,
all dusky brown and soft white,

and dark eyes that showed no guile.
He stood before me on the crumbling
asphalt, his hooves stuttering a moment

before he chose to stare in return.
Two new antlers rose thin and straight
between his ears, and I thought,

this one is bold, he wants juicy leaves,
the best fruit, he bounds up to the houses
to tear them from their branches.

When he leapt again, he was gone
completely, the morning closed around him
like a book, the book of the deer world,

written in scent and quiver and sunlight,
where the living word slips past us
before we grasp what it means.

Muir in the Woods

Eyes alert, he spots the bear just before
it bounds into a berry patch. He tucks
a crust of bread in his shirt and strides

onward, follows the river toward
Tokopah Falls. Mule deer browse,
unperturbed by his presence. He's

nearly one of them, sharing crystal air
while the last sunflowers bend their
heads. *Going out is really going in,*

he says, and he's out for days, or weeks,
lingering with the giants, speechless
in their silence. When he dozes

on the granite dome of Sunset Rock,
he dreams a sky of dirty haze,
slopes gray with dying trees.

What nightmare is this?
What travesty?
What shadow eclipsing the sun?

Becoming Sequoia

To live for thousands of years,
you can't be perturbed
by every insect or squirrel
or change in the weather.
When wildfire scorches
your skin, you heal and keep
going. Your intention protects
you like an amulet—you push
upward according to plan,
knuckled base nestled
against earth like a fist. You
follow the ways of a shaman,
transmuting air, rock, soil,
water. Your stamina could
build a world from ice.
You have no quarrel with
the sun, or with anyone—
radiating light from trunk
to crown, stretching taller
until one day, gravity takes
you down. Then, you commend
your body to the ground
among seeds already sown
and sprouting, no effort
wasted, birds and stars
sounding your name.

The Linton Yew

You have lived so long,
only the stars remember
what you know—families
of trees who fell before you,
processions of animals, insects,
birds—and humans with their
strange church of stone.
You bore witness to them all
and replied with leaves,
your canopy expanding
as your body hollowed
and began to fail. The sky
intervened, helped you
send down a root from
your crown, guide it
deep into earth to form
a new trunk—now firm
at the heart of gnarled
and twisted time, shards
of sun-dappled bole
splayed like scallop-shells
around your revival.

Temps Perdu

Winter. Time and again, I go to bed early and wake up early. While warm air blows down from the ceiling, I pore through my seed catalog. My eyes widen—what's this listing in the lettuce section? Before I can blink, it's Ojai, 1978, and I'm in the foothills behind the old stone house. Live oaks guard a dappled clearing of native plants and wildflowers, growing profusely after heavy rains. My friend points out a green bounty of Miner's lettuce. We pick and eat the sweet, tender leaves, then take home as much as we can carry. All spring I go back to the meadow and forage, feeding myself from the land.

for old time's sake
planting a packet
of happiness

The Thing with Feathers

Lit by the waning moon,
great-horned repeats his four-beat cry.
It takes all the breath in his beaked tower

to build a refrain, then keep sounding—
a long solo with a long wait to be answered.
You came into the world with that kind

of faith—said what you were born
to say, right on time, even though
you kept your life small as a mouse

while the predator swiveled his head
and watched for the run he knew
you would make, your chances

shuffling like a deck of cards—
then, just as suddenly as he arrived,
the owl leaves and you're free to go.

The Shallows

In the canyon, where time lays down
its layers to be counted, the air fills
with alarm when thunder rolls in.
No resistance is given. Rain rages
like a bonfire. Sycamore leaves
brace for the torrent, then let go.
Their journey is a prayer in the shape
of water, borne without kindness
or grief, going who knows how far,
or toward what end. Unconcerned,
a black garter snake swims the cold
current, alert for fish he will find
near the edges, the shallows made new.

Companion

Edges sharp against cobalt sky—
I know my eroded bluff
better than I know myself.

That rosy shape-shifter
remains my hourglass
sifting chameleon light.

On this earth
there's no easy duration—
shadow after shadow

breath after breath
until the moment of no-breath—
and what then?

Grain by grain
the sandstone thins
taking me with it—

II.

Mapless

The Sanctity of Reading

The words draw over me
in their cloak of beauty
and I float somewhere
above the bed, in an ether
where futures take root
and the past revises
until, well pruned,
it bears forbidden fruit.
The book falls flat on my stomach
and I could be twelve again,
barely breathing,
eyes worn from devouring
page after page,
caught in the thrill
of fabrication.
The risk is, a book
can break your life apart,
then put it back
so you barely recognize
anyone, least of all you.
But that is what all
great religions teach—
one unexpected resurrection,
and suddenly you're a believer.

Grandmother Returns to Sedona Through My Eyes

The mountains breathe
their trees lean against me—

My eyes see what
your eyes saw
you slip quietly into me—

You turn my head
and I remember
what you remember—

red rocks
ponderosa pines
the rush of water—

the sudden stroke
that broke your dream
of being an artist—

twenty-two years
in nursing homes
how you gripped my hand—

Tonight you take me down
the steep-sided canyon
to stand by the singing stream.

And this morning I pull
a single black hair
from my brown head.

Blue Beetles

—After Jane Hirshfield

In dark woods,
they worship *the god of More*—

filled with sweet liquor
of vines and leaves,

submerged on the forest floor.
They have eyes I dare not

meet in dreams—
eroded cones of light.

They ask where I look
with my twin candles,

where I go
with my wobbly hips.

They whir past my ears
toward buried treasure.

To them I'm a senseless
rumor—tree with no fruit,

stone in the sky, breath
of no consequence.

They do their work
without me.

The Interior

No one lives there—too remote,
merciless, a place for outlaws

in hiding, not meant to sustain
human life. The wind can rend

skin from flesh, the cold take
your eyes. Yet you yearn for

this waste of glacier and desert,
volcano and lake—an untamed

wilderness shaped like a heart.
Something waits for you

on the knife-edge of danger—
the chance to be someone

else. The chance you might
not return. The chance

Earth herself might sing
in a voice you can hear.

Seal Man

His home was an island, his lot a fisherman.
But not until the boat sank did he learn

how different he was. How the frigid sea
was his element, how he could swim

with the ease of a seal hour after hour,
reach the shore, climb a cliff, cross a field

of volcanic rock, barefoot, to his village.
And more—how he could talk to birds.

How ever after he looked at people
with the direct and guileless eyes

of an animal. How he could say,
I'm nothing but a small drop

in the ocean. How he found
a way to live on.

Neolithic Girl

Stone whisperer
finds human life
too fragile
for her liking

> *no farm or hut*
> *can claim her*

She prefers
a hardened skin
slips in and out
of stone-life

> *rattles strung*
> *with tooth and claw*

holds parlays
with sarsens
who journey far
then stand upright

> *gathering*
> *on grassy plains*

solstice night
starlight helps her
move through time
fold it forward

> *she sees her future*
> *fallen*

Pah-din
—Sequoia National Park

Bedrock mortars cluster
together—moon craters
on a granite boulder.

In sky-time, women
sit here, grind acorns.
Their daughters work

beside them. Nearby,
a stone face, markings
in red paint—sun-spokes,

open arms, stories
in plain sight. Below,
a path lined with oaks

and more boulders,
the roar of water.
Fish traps in narrows,

willow baskets to leach
acid from new meal.
Voices singing—

Pah-din, pah-din.
The place to go in.
This place.

A living dream.

Encounter

We saw the ancient arena in April, ringed by snow-capped mountains. That vacant circle of dirt held echoes of sound laid down over millennia. Breaking every lost rule, we wandered across the killing ground—no lions to tear us limb from limb, no onlookers shouting from stone ramparts. Only a pulsing sun.

rain of arrows
aimed straight
at the heart

Never Again

Never again to swim
with hippos in the Nile

Never again to stand
in a courtyard of pruned sycamores

Never again to stroll
past the portico's carved columns

Never again to taste
blue lotus, third eye open

Never again to wear
sheer pleated linen in moonlight

Never again to breathe
the scent of sweet-spiced *kyphi*

Never again to clap
in time to harps and flutes

Never again—
and always

Cosmic Soup

3 am breakthrough

west wind
cool air seeps
through the glass

a shaft of moonlight

mockingbird
singing the night
into myth

strikes my face

mapless
what current carried me
this far

The Leap

On the other side
of the wormhole

where space is filled
with everything
imaginable

there's a world
enough like this one
to make homesickness

stronger—a time
traveler wakes
to find herself

a stranger
her head aches
with what came before

no one believes
she's from elsewhere
eventually

she tries to forget
makes a new life
but still carries

the past in her bones
passes it on
to her children

who are restless

looking upwards
towards they know
not what

Alcyone Retold

Daughter of the wind-king,
she learned young how quickly
dead calm can turn to raging fury.

Winter brought storms, tore the sea,
flung towers of spray on the beach,
knocked her off her feet, nearly

dragging her under. She never forgot
that power. When she wed the son
of the morning star, *sweet peace*—

but in the depths, her charmed
existence churned like breaking water.
Her mate insisted on setting sail

to consult the oracle of Apollo,
sure no god would let him drown.
He ignored her warnings, left her

on shore to watch his ship drop
below the horizon. The shock
when he washed up at her feet

turned her into a kingfisher.
Inconsolable, she folded him
in her wings, kissed him with

her beak—a devotion that remade
him in her likeness, though she
claimed the brighter blue.

It was she who chose to nest
on the waves, taming them
so her young could hatch,

and so other lovers might pass
those straits unharmed.

Sea Turtle

This is an old story.
A bird and a fish fall in love,
but they cannot live together.

I felt myself crossing over,
becoming one, then the other,
laying eggs on land,
gathering food from coral.

How old am I? No one can say.
Honu, they call me, blown
by a hurricane to the bay
to drift with herds of snorkelers.

My flippers beat like wings.
They bear me to the surface
for a breath to take below.

You would have to soar
to glimpse my leathery head
above the crests of wave.

My father flew
through death's door.
My mother flailed
in a sea of tears.

And then I was born.
Alone on damp sand,
I knew where to look
and what to do.

When I sleep
the water in my body
goes in search of you.

River Daisies, River Geese

They always come back, she says.
Right to this spot.
The bank gleams with snowy petals.
He loves me, he loves me not.

Daisies fall from her hands
as the geese pass overhead.

She leaves her travail behind,
buys a ticket across the sea.
She has never seen so much sun.

She has lived long enough
to be unreasonably wanted
by someone.

She brings back a story to tell
these long winter nights:

My true love stood
on the green bank
and all that is ugly in life
flew south...

She walks or they walk together
along the river in her mind—

And the flowers say
what they always say,
We are here for the taking—

And the water waves
goodbye over rocks—
unlike the calm she came for,
a song to steal her heart.

A Long Goodbye

Winter came more suddenly
    than earth.

You were accustomed
    to the ground beneath

your feet—so familiar,
    as though it would last

forever, with you ranging
    upon it—

then this hard freeze,
    this bleak cold

that shut your eyes
    and stopped you

in mid-stride. Shorn of hope,
    you mourn the frailty

of your own form passing
    into the dark

to be remade. A rarefied
    air surrounds you,

prelude to decay—
    enough to nurture

the hurt of not existing.
    Unmoving, you wait

for the thaw—in your own
    time, on your own

terms, you dissolve
    and fall as snow.

Invoking the Salamander

So we will walk on the ruins of a vast sky,
The far-off landscape will bloom
Like a destiny in the vivid light.

The long-sought most beautiful country
Will lie before us land of salamanders.
— Yves Bonnefoy

I. Visitation

Indian summer, season of dust.
I vacuum blinds and behind
louvered doors, where I find
the salamander—tiny, lean,
built like a racecar, almost
blending into the carpet.
I take a napkin from the table,
scoop up the interloper,
shake him out the front door.
He stands on the concrete,
looking straight at me,
wide-mouthed and wide-eyed,
defiant as a boxer. I go back
inside, turn my thoughts
to the next room.

II. Dream

There's a keepsake box
I've had since childhood
but never look into.
The lid lifts. A giant
white salamander slips out,
quickly hiding where
she can't be found.
Of this earth, yet not

of this earth—a hidden
life, untended, survives
on air, and finally stirs.

Someone holds a gun
to my head. I am strangely
calm despite the threat,
the cold kiss of the barrel,
the menacing strangers
in an unknown room, doing
what they think they must—
what I think they must—
since this is my dream.

Or is it?

I feel something
dreaming outside me,
an ether of swirls and eddies,
a rushing stream of intent.

Somewhere the salamander
waits, careful teacher,
patient survivor—
pale as the ash of a pyre,
fearsome arbiter of fate.

III. Origins

When Earth and its magic
were younger, people trembled
before the salamander:

Eater of fire.
Birther of gods.
Bestower of visions.
Smiter of ignorance.

Mistress of transformation,
bridging earth and water.
Mistress of disguise,
portal to soul memories.

The salamander speaks
in the hiss of a match,
the crackling blaze,
the spent coals. Those
who follow the changeling
across the threshold
remember each incarnation.
They know the alchemists' gold.

IV. Invitation

The dark-haired, dark-skinned woman
bows her head. She does not look
this way. The day's work waits
to be done. She walks steadily
over the ridge and down the arroyo.

I've tried to see more, but it feels
made up, a reflection not of her,
but of me. She looks back, laughs,
teases, leading me somewhere
I'm not sure I want to be led.

Her arm moves in a circle,
slow and deliberate, a ritual.
There is a trail. Others to go with.
Food is prepared by women
silent as stones, smiling
like pebbles in water.

Time passes and we return,
she and I, to the place where she

walks away and I don't follow.
Yet each time I go a step farther.

V. Journey

The tiny salamander reappears,
runs circles around the foyer.
How he gets in is a mystery.
Released to the backyard,
he vanishes into nature.

The great white remains at large.
But in the poet's papers, sheet
after sheet, ceremony stones
fall into place, feet blaze
the path ahead, lungs expand
into deathless space, each word
an open mouth that demands:
Burn. Defy. Rise. Leap.

III.

Mercy Seat

Ode to a Pear

Do you remember
the tree where you were born
at the far end of the world?

You left your orchard
in the Alto Valle
crossed continents and oceans
flew higher than swallows
to land in California
on my kitchen counter
your perfect flesh
ripening with a blush.

In the time of COVID
you upturn seasons
autumn Bartlett
in Mojave spring.

I can hardly grasp
you're from Argentina,
can't help but think
of the energy spent
to bring you here—
how humans
take and take
to satisfy a craving.

Like you I exist
in this moment
then the next
as long as life
will last—and soon
dentro de poco
you'll be part of me.

Doctor, My Eyes

My hummingbird friend fans her wings in the spray from the hose. Then she settles on a yucca spear not a foot from my face. We like each other. We like these quiet moments together. Gazing, and breathing. Gazing, and breathing.

august dawn
the cool of the day
evaporates

Mourning the Doves

I hear them less and less.
Their racket used to arrive

at dawn, follow me from
room to room—now I fill

water dishes and wait
for their descent—the flutter,

the chase, the parables—
but there are no five-note calls,

and the doves who do come
are smaller, darker, landing

at sunset and roosting in silence.
Do they even know the refrain

that drove me crazy,
that I finally came to love,

that used to remind me
what I have to do?

Escape

I enter the garden and latch the door—
only to find a moth in the enclosure
with me, a siren I step closer

to admire—nearly her undoing, since,
panicked, she tries to force an exit
through half-inch wire mesh,

and won't stop, even when I open
the door. When she breaks free,
she's wounded, barely hanging on—

leaving me sorry for my curiosity,
for crossing the divide between us.
Yet her flurry feels familiar.

How often have I let fear drive
an action that injured my life,
when I had a wide berth to fly?

I'll never know the answer,
there at the edge of awareness,
sky just out of reach.

Needed Elsewhere

The sleeping earth saw no sign
of a storm, until, before dawn,
a soundless sky flashed white,
then white again, electricity
seeking an outlet. That energy
formed a jagged bolt, struck
a single Joshua tree, reduced
it to a cinder. Were those
ragged arms needed elsewhere,
to hold something unnamed,
in a place without bodies?

The Last of Their Kind

White wolverines aren't supposed to exist. So I'm startled to come across two in the woodsy undergrowth. A hunter, already gone, beheaded the larger and took the pelt. Furious, the severed head snaps and snarls, biting the air and its fellow wolverine, who is smaller but equally fierce. A struggle ensues, both claiming victory before succumbing to their wounds.

desperate times—
the storm's breath
shivers my neck

Overnight at White Pocket

You doze if you can, a blanket
of cold stars pulled over your head—

then get up before dawn to catch
the first rays lighting those pale

and painted rocks—swirled concretions
of bygone dunes, shaped by wind

and snow and rain, like the storm
that blew in yesterday, casting

kaleidoscopes of shadow and sun
over gnarled domes and ridges,

a few black cattle passing through—
caught in geologic time, you watch

waves of sandstone ebb and flow
until you're submerged among

the moqui marbles—
wherever your breath has gone,

you're not the same as when you came.

Trail Chains

you inch your way
along the precipice
hand over hand

whatever it takes
for the view
and the thrill

of that precarious
balance—
traversing

the vertical cliff
towards your new
sense of self

the edge between
flying and falling
intact

you cling
to the shadow side
pull toward the light

slick stones underfoot
faint clouds overhead—
don't look down

as you round
the last curve
just hold your breath

facing into the wind

Winter Solstice

primeval

>>> last light
>>> the looming blackness
>>> of pines

these aching roots

>>> new moon sky
>>> Orion cinches
>>> his belt

of my bones

>>> curtains of snow
>>> an unseen raven
>>> knocking

Gideon's Bluff

High walls, no visible windows, treeless grounds—this rest home
has the look and feel of a fortress. Racks of brochures, no reception
desk. I wander about the empty lobby. When a staffer finally
appears, she eyes me and remarks, *You look old enough.* I shoot back,
Younger than you might expect.

blood-red cliffs—
where will I go when the years
catch up with me

Worlds Apart

—After a painting by Kendall Johnson

When you talk about dark and light,
what do you mean? No one wants
to be remembered for the worst
thing they did. The swirling universe

between two people is infinite,
yet there's a meeting ground—
the gray zone of forgiveness, where
no man's as bad as he seems.

Didn't you sense how this would end?
You surrounded yourself with darkness
when I knew you were made of light.
You took on my darkness so I might

continue. You watched me across
a gulf of stars while I became a ghost.
If I could have loved you, I might
have saved myself from this fate.

If you could have loved me,
none of this would have happened.

For Helena

Trees and stars
need a certain distance

to thrive—no closer.
You taught me this,

planting seeds in the shape
of constellations.

I'm a clumsy learner
with good intentions—

uprooting mistakes
and starting over.

I get there eventually—
patient, watchful,

you beam on.

This Changes Everything

From time out of mind, calling a Deep Witness has been a last resort. Dressed in black, androgynous, they enter unobtrusively, eyes cast downward—yet no one present can escape their gaze. They stand silent, radiating lasers of truth, changing everyone around them. Feuds fall apart, poisoned lifeways dissolve, the tyranny of the familiar vanishes as though it never existed. Those affected are faced with starting over, finding a way to live without falsehoods, groping along the lines of their breath.

mountain path
just when you need it
a mercy seat

Arrival

here is the light
that allows another
day to happen

every living thing
leans toward that beam
from the east

golden after
the grey of dawn
a slight breeze

stirring branches
and leaves—
this is what

we came for
the light riding
higher

lengthening
shadows
behind us

Cynthia Anderson has published a dozen poetry collections, including *Full Circle* (Cholla Needles Arts & Literary Library, 2022) and *The Missing Peace* (Velvet Dusk Publishing, 2021). Her poems frequently appear in journals and anthologies, and her work has been nominated for the Pushcart Prize and Best of the Net. Cynthia is co-editor of the anthology *A Bird Black As the Sun: California Poets on Crows & Ravens*. She has lived in California for over 40 years. www.cynthiaandersonpoet.com

Sheila-Na-Gig Editions

www.ingramcontent.com/pod-product-compliance
Lightning Source LLC
Chambersburg PA
CBHW060353130626
46553CB00003B/1205